√15

SCIENCE FAIR
SUCCESS!

Kirsten W. Larson

Rourke
Educational Media

rourkeeducationalmedia.com

Before Reading:

Building Academic Vocabulary and Background Knowledge

Before reading a book, it is important to tap into what your child or students already know about the topic. This will help them develop their vocabulary, increase their reading comprehension, and make connections across the curriculum.

1. Look at the cover of the book. What will this book be about?
2. What do you already know about the topic?
3. Let's study the Table of Contents. What will you learn about in the book's chapters?
4. What would you like to learn about this topic? Do you think you might learn about it from this book? Why or why not?
5. Use a reading journal to write about your knowledge of this topic. Record what you already know about the topic and what you hope to learn about the topic.
6. Read the book.
7. In your reading journal, record what you learned about the topic and your response to the book.
8. After reading the book complete the activities below.

Content Area Vocabulary

Read the list. What do these words mean?

analyze
assume
communicates
control
data
dependent variable
design
develop
engineering
experiment
hazardous
hypothesis
independent variable
limitations
observe
process
prototype
research
variable

After Reading:

Comprehension and Extension Activity

After reading the book, work on the following questions with your child or students in order to check their level of reading comprehension and content mastery.

1. Why are displays needed for your science fair project? (Asking questions)
2. What are some ways you can get ideas for a science fair? (Summarize)
3. What is data? (Summarize)
4. If the tests conducted for your science experiment can go against your hypothesis, what is the importance of science fairs? (Infer)
5. What ideas do you have for a science fair project? (Text to self connection)

Extension Activity

You are going to create a display at your science fair involving plants and water. What could your hypothesis be? What are some ways you can test your hypothesis? What data are you looking to collect? What limitations might you have? What could you research? Create an outline for your experiment.

Table of Contents

CHAPTER ONE

Get Ready for the Science Fair

You see the flyer on a bulletin board in the cafeteria: School Science Fair on March 15. Science rocks. Fairs are fun, and March is a couple of months away. There's plenty of time to plan. You would sign up, if you could just figure out what a science fair is.

Participants share their projects at science fairs.

A science fair is simply a show-and-tell. You **develop** a project over several weeks. The fair is the grand finale. It's your chance to show off your work to friends, family, and judges. Students compete at schools, at the state level, and even internationally. Some science fairs happen online. If you have a winning project, you might receive a scholarship or other prizes.

The science fair starts with a project. It's your chance to be a scientist or engineer. You pick a question to explore or a problem to solve. These might be, "What do plants need to grow?" or "How can I build a faster go-kart?"

Then you do some **research**. You make an educated guess. To test that guess, you develop an **experiment** or model. Sometimes you can even team up with your best buddies, for more fun.

When you work with a partner, you get twice as many ideas about how to make your project a success.

Science projects come in several shapes and sizes. Say "science fair," and most people think of test tubes and lab experiments. But there are other types of projects too. **Engineering** projects let you improve an existing product or machine. Imagine modifying a go-kart so it goes even faster! In some cases, you may invent something completely new.

There are other opportunities too. Computer buffs can write new programs. Math whizzes can solve a problem. The key is to create a project that uses your talents and your interests.

The recipe for science fair success has just a few simple ingredients: a topic you care about and a question you can test. You will spend a lot of time on your project, so pick a subject that interests you. If you are a basketball fanatic, find out what drills make better players. If you love airplanes, make one that flies farther. Your enthusiasm will shine through. And it could make you a winner.

Pick a topic that will utilize the skills and knowledge you already have.

Your experiment or engineering **design** are your test. These tests produce **data**, or information you can collect and measure. For example, it would be hard to answer the question, "Which go-kart is the best?" But you could ask which design is fastest. Your data would be the test times on the track.

Time your laps on a race track to collect data for go-kart speed.

When it comes to getting ready for the fair, there's no time to waste. Projects can take a few weeks or a couple of months. Start with your deadline and work backward. The school science fair is March 15, so a sample schedule might look like this:

Science Fair Step	Time It Will Take	Deadline
Turn in project		March 15
Create display	1 week	March 8
Analyze results	1 week	March 1
Conduct experiment	2 weeks (this may vary)	February 15
Design experiment	1 week	February 8
Pick a topic, develop hypothesis	2 weeks	January 25

CHAPTER TWO

Brainstorm Ideas

The first thing to do is pick a topic. Think about things you like to do outside of school. Perhaps basketball gets your blood pumping. Maybe you're a budding baker or video gamer. Make a list of five to ten hobbies or interests in a notebook. Don't discount any ideas just yet.

Any interest you have may spark an idea for a science project. Ask questions about how to make an improvement, and turn that into an experiment.

If your list is short, take a field trip. Maybe there's a museum or science center that could spark an idea. Or, head to your local library and browse the nonfiction titles. Look at books about science, nature, math, and engineering. If something looks interesting, add that subject to your list.

Another way to generate ideas is to take a walk outside and **observe**. Maybe you see a group of ants lugging a piece of food. Perhaps you notice a plastic shopping bag caught in a tree. Pull out your notebook and describe the scene. Focus only on what's happening, not what might be causing it.

Now ask yourself questions about what you observed. How much can a single ant carry? Are ants picky eaters? Could shopping bags be made of materials that break down?

As you jot down ideas in your notebook, consider any **limitations** you might have. Workspace may be one. Ants may not be welcome in the house. Making new shopping bags may require a chemistry lab. If you're designing a go-kart, you may need a workshop with room to build and test your designs.

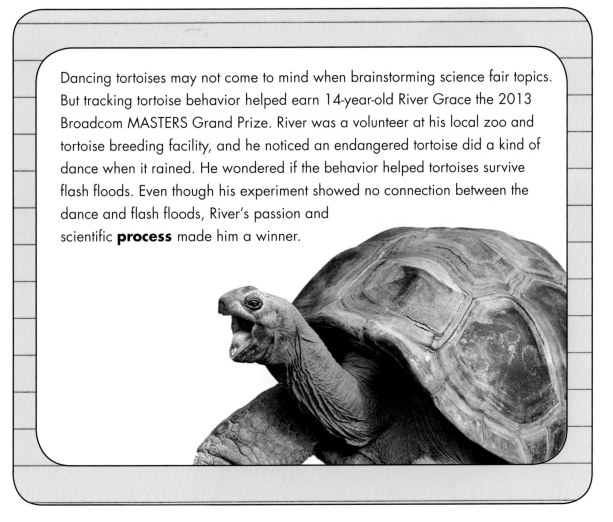

Dancing tortoises may not come to mind when brainstorming science fair topics. But tracking tortoise behavior helped earn 14-year-old River Grace the 2013 Broadcom MASTERS Grand Prize. River was a volunteer at his local zoo and tortoise breeding facility, and he noticed an endangered tortoise did a kind of dance when it rained. He wondered if the behavior helped tortoises survive flash floods. Even though his experiment showed no connection between the dance and flash floods, River's passion and scientific **process** made him a winner.

Time might be another limiting factor. If the science fair is only a couple of weeks away, you can't grow plants. Money could also drive your decisions. Make a list of what you need and how much it costs. Also, some fairs require special permission to do tests on animals or people. Toxic chemicals or living tissue projects need to be approved before you start. Always check your fair's requirements.

Write down any limiting factors next to your ideas. This will help you narrow down your list.

CHAPTER THREE

Ask the Question

Now it's time to turn your topic into a science question to see if you can test it. Let's look at an example. Outside you notice plants in the shade dying. But plants in sunny spots grow green and healthy. You wonder, "Does light affect how plants grow?"

What caused one plant to die and the other one grow? Make a guess and test your guess in an experiment.

Make an educated guess about the answer. This guess, based on what you know, is your **hypothesis**. These guesses usually take the form "If..., then..." Your hypothesis could be: If plants get more light, then they will grow taller. You can measure the plants' height to learn if your guess was right or wrong. Congratulations, you have a question you can test!

DOES MORE LIGHT = BIGGER PLANT?

Engineering projects have a slightly different question. Engineers ask, "How can I make it better?" You may have noticed that go-karts are low and wide with tiny tires. How does this design help them drive fast? You ask, "How can I build a better go-kart?"

First you must research existing go-kart designs. Think about the strengths and weaknesses of each one. You find that you can improve the tires. If you can race the old and new designs against each other, you have a question you can test.

Research has an important role at this stage. You need to know what other scientists have learned about your subject. Checking out books or looking for science papers on the Internet are a good start. You'll need to **examine** existing designs for your engineering project.

Before designing an experiment, you will want to know as much about your topic as possible.

Finding good science sources is a tough job. At the library, rely on librarians to steer you to good sources. When using the Internet, know who wrote the information. Use websites from colleges and universities, science centers, newspapers, and science magazines. Also, talking to a scientist or engineer is a great way to research your project. A teacher or relative may be a good resource. Or, contact a local college to find a science advisor.

CHAPTER FOUR

Design Your Project

Science question. Check. Hypothesis. Check. Now's the time to write down exactly how you'll test your guess. This step-by-step process is known as a procedure.

Jot down anything that could change in your experiment. These are the variables.

First Treat Both Plants the Same

Plant A

Plant B

Plant A	Plant B
Days 1-7	Days 1-7
Plant A receives 6 hours of sunlight per day.	Plant B receives 6 hours of sunlight per day.

For a successful experiment, you should only change one **variable** at a time. This way you can tell which variable caused a specific change.

Then Change the Variable

Plant A   *Plant B*

Plant A	Plant B
Days 8-21	Days 8-21
Plant A receives 4 hours of sunlight per day.	Plant B receives 6 hours of sunlight per day.
	variable

Light Is the Variable

Your plant hypothesis was, "If plants get more light, then they will grow taller." Light should be the one and only variable you change. The variable you change on purpose is your **independent variable**.

The height of the plants will change too. Plant height is a **dependent variable.** That's the variable you measure. Write down your dependent variable and how you will measure it in your notebook.

In order to be sure about this cause and effect relationship, you need to keep everything else exactly the same.

Plant Height Is the Dependent Variable

Plant A   *Plant B*

The Plant without Sunlight Is the Control

If a plant is placed in the shade of a tall tree, it will not get much sunlight.

Finally you need a point of comparison. The easiest thing is to leave out your key ingredient, which is light. If three plants in a sunny spot grow tall and healthy, while the one in the shade doesn't, you know light affected growth. The plant without the key ingredient is the **control**.

Also consider how many times you must test your experiment to prove your hypothesis. Growing just bean seeds with different amounts of light may not be enough. Sunlight may affect bean seed height, but you can't **assume** it's the same for all plants. Each time you test the experiment is called a **trial**. Write down the number of trials you'll perform.

Compare the Trials

Trial One

Trial Two

Trial Three

27

Engineering projects also require a procedure. If you're building a better go-kart by changing to larger tires, tire size is the independent variable. Race times are the dependent variable, which is the effect of the changes you make. Everything else must be the same, including your track length, how hard you push the cars during the test, and other pieces of the go-kart design. Your control would be the standard go-kart design with small tires.

Consider the number of trials you'll run. You could run each car three times on a straight track. Then you add a slight curve and run each car three more times. Finally, you add a steep curve and test the cars. With two go-kart designs, three track configurations, and three runs per configuration, you'll have 18 trials.

You sketched your design and purchased your materials. Now build your **prototype** and test it against the device you are trying to improve. Which performed better? Graph your results to find patterns in the data.

Draw different versions of your idea to get an idea of how it will work.

Engineering design is a circular process. Your first design may not be any better than the original design. In this case, you may want to make improvements and retest it. You may do this several times before you are happy with your work.

Go-Kart Trails

	Car A	Car B
Trial 1	38.0 seconds	36.8 seconds
Trial 2	37.2 seconds	37.4 seconds
Trial 3	39.1 seconds	36.1 seconds

Analyze the data from your trials to decide if your design is an improvement.

CHAPTER FIVE

Show Your Data

You prepped. You planned. You prepared. Now you do the experiment. As you do each trial, record your observations. For the plants, measure how tall they are every few days. Keep a log of the measurements in a science notebook.

Day	Plant A Height	Plant B Height
Monday	2 inches	3 inches
Wednesday	2.25 inches	3.5 inches

Once you've completed your experiment, look for patterns in the data. Graphs are helpful. Use graph paper or a computer with graphing software. You could plot the amount of light the plants received each day along the bottom and plant height along the side.

Ask yourself questions about your results. Are they what you expected? Could something else explain the same results? Do you have any results that don't fit the pattern? Why? Talking with a science teacher or scientist can help you explain your results.

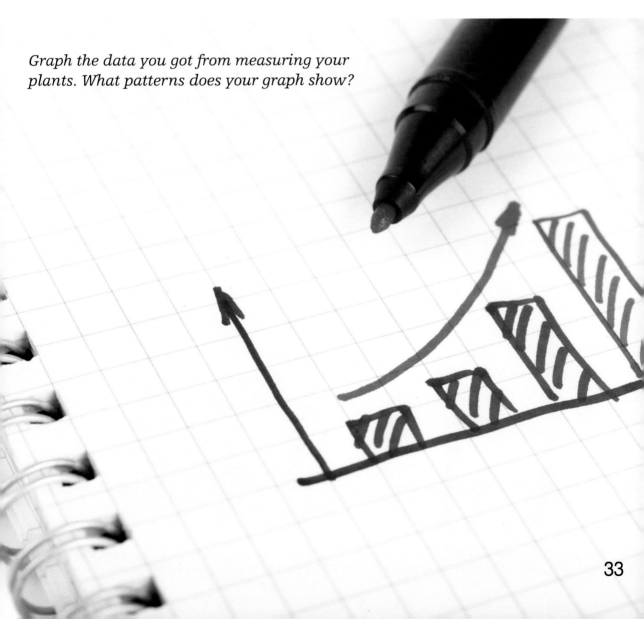

Graph the data you got from measuring your plants. What patterns does your graph show?

Keeping a detailed science notebook is critical. Fair judges will leaf through your data log, so make sure your handwriting is at its best. Common choices are a composition or spiral notebook. You might pick looseleaf paper and a binder. Computer-savvy students could keep an online notebook. Also take pictures or video of your experiment to capture your setup. These can be a part of your display.

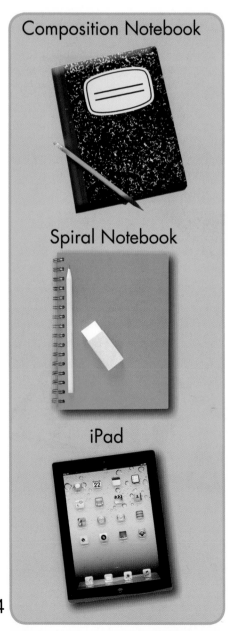

Composition Notebook

Spiral Notebook

iPad

Days 8-21

Car A, Trial 2

When analyzing results, you may learn that you were way off base. That's okay. Getting it wrong is how scientists learn. You can contribute to science even when your answer is not what you expected. And you just might become a science fair winner too.

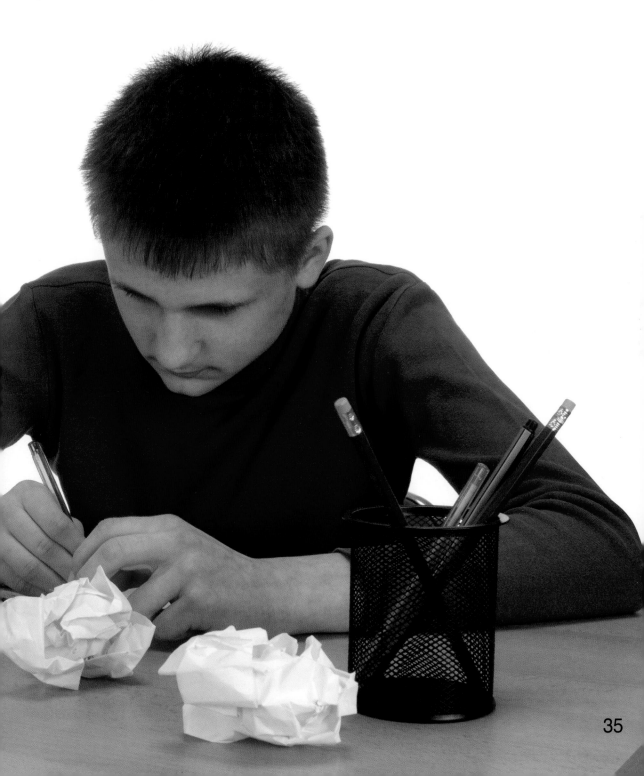

CHAPTER SIX

On Display

Your display **communicates** your process and findings to the judges. It must tell them everything they need to know about your project. Most fairs have similar display guidelines. But before you start cutting and pasting, check your fair's specific rules.

Trifold poster boards from craft stores are common. Organize your information from left to right. The left side describes background information, your question and hypothesis, your procedure, and your materials. The right side has your discussion and conclusion. The middle features your project title, photos of your experiment, graphs, and results.

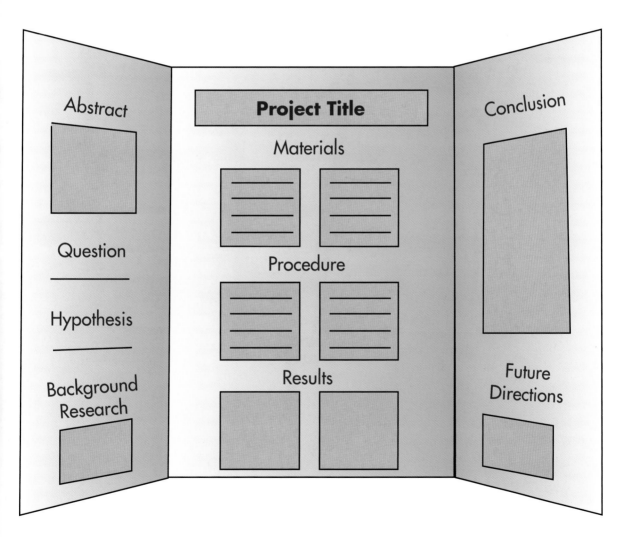

Organize your information clearly so that the judges will get a clear understanding of your work.

Middle school fairs often require a research paper. While your display is a visual summary of your project, the paper provides a written overview. Judges can read your paper for more information if you're not standing by your display to answer questions.

Stapling your research paper and placing it flat on the table is fine. For more impact, give it a report cover, bind it, or even place it on a stand

Remember, your display should be eye-catching, but it's not an arts and crafts project. Here are some do's and don'ts for developing dynamic displays:

- Use a computer to create your headings, paragraphs, and graphs.
- Use easy-to-read fonts like Times New Roman, Arial, or Helvetica.
- Paragraphs should be 14-point font size for easiest reading.
- Headings should be large enough to read from several feet away. The project titles should be about 3 inches (7.62 centimeters) tall.
- Use clear, crisp photos to show your setup.

CHAPTER SEVEN

At the Science Fair

Science fairs come in all shapes and sizes. Some take place in the school cafeteria. Others occur only on the computer. All give you a chance to share your experiment, make friends, and have fun.

School Fairs

Schools often hold fairs during the spring. These make great first fairs. Some school fairs declare winners. Others award all participants.

County and State Fairs

These fairs may bring together thousands of students from a region or state. Any student may enter a county fair, but in order to enter a state fair, students often must win at a county or regional fair first.

National and International Fairs

The premiere middle school science fair is the Broadcom MASTERS. Before entering the MASTERS, students must compete successfully at a county or state fair affiliated with the competition. Two finalists from this fair then go on to compete against students from eleven other countries.

Virtual Fairs

Your schedule may be packed with sports, music lessons, and other activities. If you can't spare time for the local fair, an online science fair may be right for you. The Google Science Fair and the International Science and Technology Fair are two great virtual fairs to check out.

You may not have to sign up for your school fair. But other fairs require you to register. Your school must sign up first.

To register you need your snappy project title and a 250-word abstract, which is a summary of your project. If your project involves an experiment on certain animals, humans, living tissues, or **hazardous** chemicals, you must show prior approval.

Large fairs can last several days. You set up on the first day. On the second day, you meet with judges to showcase your project. On the final day, the fair opens to the public. All your friends can come see your display. An awards ceremony caps off the day. Follow these simple tips for smooth science fair sailing.

- **What to wear:** Nice slacks or a simple skirt with a collared shirt or blouse will fit the bill.

- **Mind your manners:** When meeting judges, introduce yourself, shake hands, and smile. Look them in the eye while talking.

- **Practice makes perfect:** Explain your project to parents, teachers, and friends. The more you've rehearsed, the more confident you'll feel.

- **You're the expert:** The judges don't know anything about your project. Remember that when it comes to your project, you're the pro.

In elementary school, science fair judges are usually parents, teachers, and other community members. At higher-level fairs, scientists and engineers in different disciplines serve as judges. No matter who the judges are, they look for creativity, scientific process, thoroughness, and a clear display and explanation from you.

Judges, especially scientists and engineers, can provide valuable feedback about your project.

Your head swirls with ideas. But you now know what science fairs are all about. It's time to take a deep breath and dive right in. You just may be a science fair winner too.

Glossary

analyze (AN-uh-lize): to examine something thoroughly to understand it

assume (uh-SOOM): to suppose something is true

communicates (kuh-MYOO-ni-kates): to share information

control (kuhn-TROHL): an experimental group that serves as a comparison, allowing you to see the effect of your independent variable

data (DAY-tuh): information collected from an experiment

dependent variable (di-PEN-duhnt VAIR-ee-uh-buhl): what is measured in an experiment; the part of the experiment that may change

design (di-ZINE): to draw up a plan for something

develop (di-VEL-up): to create something over time

engineering (en-juh-NEER-ing): designing machines or structures

experiment (ik-SPER-uh-muhnt): to perform a scientific test to learn something new

hazardous (HAZ-ur-duhs): dangerous

hypothesis (hye-PAH-thi-sis): a statement that can be tested through a scientific procedure

independent variable (in-di-PEN-duhnt VAIR-ee-uh-buhl): the variable that you have control of and purposefully change during an experiment

limitations (lim-i-TAY-shuhns): something that prevents you from completing an activity

observe (uhb-ZURV): to watch something closely

process (PRAH-ses): a series of actions in a procedure

prototype (PROH-tuh-tipe): the first version of a device

research (ri-SURCH): to collect information

variable (VAIR-ee-uh-buhl): in science, something that changes

Index

Websites to Visit

http://www.sciencebuddies.org/science-fair-projects/project_scientific_
method.shtml

http://www.nasa.gov/audience/foreducators/plantgrowth/reference/
Scientific_Method.html#.UsYFdGRDs40

https://student.societyforscience.org/broadcom-masters

About the Author

Kirsten W. Larson spent six years at NASA before writing for young people. She's met Curiosity's twin, the test rover, and worked with NASA's DC-8 crews during science missions. Her articles appear in ASK, ODYSSEY, AppleSeeds, and Boys' Quest. She lives with her husband and two sons near Los Angeles, California.

photo credit: Jayma Hollister

Meet The Author!
www.meetREMauthors.com

www.rourkeeducationalmedia.com

PHOTO CREDITS: Cover and Title Page © Tpopova, Sergeyklezner, miljko, Ivcandy; page 4 © wavebreakmedia; page 5 © Jani Bryson; page 6 © Steve Debenport; page 7, 20 © Monkey Business Photography, fstop123; page 8 © Vikram Raghuvanshi; page 9 © AarStudio; page 10 © kali9; page 11 © Meda Pixel; page 12 © R. Gino Santa Maria; page 13 © Suprijono Suharjoto; page 14 © Maridav; page 15 © smileus; page 16 © Odua Images; page 17, 18, 22, 23, 24, 25, 27 © Elitsa, page 18, 25 © 9comback; page 19 © jaggat Rashidi; page 21 © Alina555; page 26 © titer84; page 30 © ammza12, Jolita Marcinkene; page 31 © Aaron Amat; page 32 © hocus-focus; page 33 © Artem Gorohov1; page 34 © pictac, KonovalikovAndrey, Aletia, Akekokssomdream; page 35 © ajt; page 36, 42, 44 © Aviahuismanphotography; page 38 © Aviahuismanphotography,; page 39 © littleny; page 41 © VikramRaghuvanski; page 43 © Stltelea; page 45 © Dragon Images

Edited by: Jill Sherman

Cover design by: Tara Raymo
Interior design by: Jen Thomas

Library of Congress PCN Data

Science Fair Success! / Kirsten W. Larson
(Let's Explore Science)
ISBN 978-1-62717-747-4 (hard cover)
ISBN 978-1-62717-869-3 (soft cover)
ISBN 978-162717-979-9 (e-Book)
Library of Congress Control Number: 2014935672

Also Available as: